How to Grow Rich
with Property Investment?

Principles and Strategies to Create Wealth
& Passive Income the Smart Way

By

Praveen Kumar & Prashant Kumar

"Ninety percent of all millionaires become so through owning real estate."

~Andrew Carnegie

TABLE OF CONTENTS

WHY INVEST IN REAL ESTATE?

To understand the power of real estate investing, you have to first understand the 'Why' of real estate. It is the 'Why' that will provide you the motivation and the energy to invest in real estate. Once you are convinced that real estate is one of the best vehicles of wealth creation, understanding the 'How' becomes easy.

"Real estate is an imperishable asset, ever increasing in value. It is the most solid security that human ingenuity has devised. It is the basis of all security and about the only indestructible security."

~Russell Sage

Most people who lack an understanding of real estate will tell you that investing in shares gives you better returns than those that come from real estate. There are others who say that renting is cheaper than buying your own house. You have to understand how real estate compares with other investment avenues such as savings account, shares/stocks, commodities and businesses.

Rate of Return

Return on investment (ROI) is definitely one of the most important criteria you should consider whilst making an investment decision. However, simplistic calculations based on yields can be very misleading.

Yield, by definition, is the ratio of annual income generated by the investment divided by the dollar amount of investment.

Rate of return should be considered after taking into account the risk involved: is the investment is inflation adjusted? Is there any capital growth on the principal invested? Does the investment provide tax benefits and is it possible to leverage your money to get higher returns?

Real estate investments – as compared to bank deposits – are definitely superior in terms of yield and capital appreciation. Savings in banks do not provide hedge against inflation and your money depreciates in value over a period of time.

Shares and stocks are perceived to have higher returns than property and provide hedge against inflation, but they are pale in comparison to real estate when you take into account the leveraging power of real estate investing and tax advantages of property. It is possible to buy properties by using Other People's Money (OPM) with returns that are 20–100 percent or more per annum.

Financial Leverage

No one has ever become rich without applying the power of leverage. Financial leverage in the investment world comes from the use of OPM or Other People's Money. In real estate investing, we buy property on a 10% down payment and yet we control 100% of real estate.

For example, let us say we buy a property of $100,000 on $10,000 down payment. Let us assume that the rent from the property covers the mortgage payments and the outgoings. If the price of property moves up by 10% over the year, the market value will increase to $110,000. This means that we would have made a profit of $10,000 on our investment of $10,000, which is a 100% return on investment and was made possible only because of the power of leverage.

Our return on investment would have been infinite had we bought the property with no down payment. This kind of financial leverage is only possible if you invest in real estate. But before you rush to buy your property with no money down, you must understand how leverage works. There is no greater leverage in life than the leverage of knowledge.

It is extremely difficult to finance other types of investments such as stock and businesses because funding is always an issue. Banks love property because of the low risk and capital appreciation associated with real estate.

Leverage can be used for quick wealth creation. If you know how to use leverage, you do not need large amounts of initial capital to start your real estate investment portfolio.

Buy Below Market Value

You must have heard the saying: *"you make money when you buy,"* and not at the time of selling. Is it possible to buy stocks or diamonds, commodity or gold below value? When you buy $100,000 worth of stock, you pay $100,000 in cash.

Investing in real estate after gaining a bit of knowledge, you can buy properties that are 10 or 20 percent, or even more below market value. There are many reasons why people sell their properties below value. You can amass great wealth by simply buying property below market value.

Increase Value of Investment

Can you increase the value of your stock or bank deposit by tinkering with it? There is simply no mechanism by which you can increase the value of your stock or any other investment because you do not control them. However, you can greatly increase the market value of your investment property by spending a small amount of money on making cosmetic changes or applying for a change in the use of property or zoning.

Investment Risk

Banks are perceived to have the least risk when compared to other investments but of late this confidence has been shattered due to the high rate of failure of banks.

Stocks carry a much higher risk because their values fluctuate on a minute to minute basis. Stocks also do not go up in value, and business disasters – like Enron – can have a nasty effect on your stock market wealth plan.

Investing in businesses can be very profitable if you know what you are doing. The failure rate of new start-up businesses is around 80%. In business, you invest in people and ideas which are usually not as solid as bricks and mortars.

Property, on the other hand, goes up in value slowly and steadily. This is proven by the record of past 300 hundred years when property values have consistently doubled every 8 to 12 years. In the market crash of 2008-2009, when the stocks nosedived to 50–80% of their value and wiped out the fortunes of millions of people—real estate prices went down by 5-30% of their value.

If you wish to understand risks, then just check what banks are willing to lend their money for – are they willing to loan money to buy paintings, antiques, diamonds, mutual funds, CDs, commodities, stocks & businesses? If so, what level of funding is available? For properties, banks will easily lend to 70-90% and in some cases, even 100% of the value. Banks are the most risk adverse institutions and if they are willing to invest in real estate up to 100% of value, then they consider the investment risk to be extremely low when compared to other investments. You should take your cue from banks.

Control over Investment

When you invest in stocks, you have no control over your investment until and unless you have the controlling shares in a company. You can hand over your money to a fund manager but you still do not have any control, and are at mercy of the competence or incompetence of the fund manager.

Shakespeare rightly said, "**Fool and his money are soon parted**." There are many Madoffs in this world waiting to rip you off your hard earned money.

Invest in real estate and you have full control over your assets. You are not at someone else's mercy—you control the shots and have peace of mind.

Real Estate Investing is forgiving to Mistakes

In every investment decision you make, there are chances of making mistakes. No one has a crystal ball that can predict the future. When compared to other vehicles of investment, real estate is very forgiving to mistakes. Property prices tend to increase relatively smoothly and consistently. The rise in property price will cover any mistake you make. Real estate investment is the simplest, most reliable and most consistent vehicle of wealth creation. You can convert even a little bit of financial IQ into lot of cold hard cash. And above all, you have total control over your investment and assets. There are no Madoffs who can run away with your hard earned money.

Real Estate Offers Exceptional Tax Advantages

The biggest expense in your lifetime is the taxes you pay to the government: I must repeat once again! You will find that you pay more than 50% of your earnings to the government in the form of taxes. Most people are not even aware of how much they pay because some taxes are indirect taxes.

The rich are rich because they pay little or no taxes. If you are smart, you can do the same and fund your lifestyle and investments by saving on the taxes.

Real estate tax laws differ from one country to another. However, universally applied tax principles throughout the world hugely favor those who invest in properties. As opposed to other investments, you can run your property investment as a business and claim back depreciation, interest payments and other expenses as a part of your business.

It is sufficient to say that tax refunds from real estate investments provide you with additional cash flow to buy more investment properties and create residual income.

In case of stocks and shares, you have very little or no tax benefits and have to pay tax on interest and dividends received. Governments at times give incentives when you invest in certain types of infrastructure bonds or mutual funds. These normally offer very low returns and many times do not justify investing in these instruments even after taking tax breaks on offer; this unique advantage makes investing in real estate very attractive when compared to other investment opportunities.

Monitoring Your Investment

Unlike other investments, you do not have to monitor your real estate investment from moment to moment like a hawk—there is peace of mind.

The whole point of investing is to create multiple streams of residual income that can fund your lifestyle. There is no fun if you have to monitor your investment on an hourly or daily basis, which is the case with investments in stocks, foreign currency or commodities, the values of which change constantly. You have to watch these investments like a hawk if you have to succeed.

Property prices tend to move very slowly, smoothly and constantly with minimum amount of fluctuations. This makes it very easy to monitor your real estate investment.

Invest in real estate and you will have the most passive and hands-free of all available investments opportunities.

Fluctuations to National Average

The price of each stock fluctuates on its own merit and there are numerous imponderable variables that dictate the price of a stock. It is therefore very difficult to monitor every stock in your portfolio because each one is very different from the other. It requires a genius of Warren Buffet's caliber to beat the market averages consistently. Even expert fund managers struggle to keep up with market averages.

In the case of real estate, fluctuations of any one property relative to the national average are very low. It requires very little expertise to beat the national average for property and increase your return on investment.

Real Estate is without doubt the safest way to create long-term residual income.

Cash Flow from Property Investment

Many people buy property with the hope of creating passive cash flow in hopes of retiring peacefully. Sometimes, they get disappointed because their properties do not generate adequate cash flow to retire even after they have bought 5 to 10 properties. The problem arises because they buy negatively geared properties that are highly leveraged. In order to create residual income, you have to buy cash flow properties and reduce your mortgage over a period of time.

Properties take time to create residual income. As time goes by the prices and rents go up: these two factors will increase your equity and cash flow. You can also convert equity into cash flow to create residual income.

Also do not confuse property flipping, forex, commodity or share trading as instruments for creating residual income.

These are nothing but full-time jobs with little or no chance of building an asset or generating residual cash flow. These activities are nothing but skill-based jobs in which you have to work full-time to make money. They may be great strategies for generating cash flow but cannot be termed as investments for creating residual income.

I hope you are convinced by now that real estate is the perhaps the best vehicle to generate long-term passive income – it is solid and time tested. We shall now examine some of the fundamental principles of real estate investing.

Real Estate Investing - Basic Principles

The most common mistake while investing in property is that people buy with their emotions. They buy in the wrong place for all the wrong reasons.

They buy property based on:

- Opinion of people who have no knowledge of investing

- In a place they were born

- They love to buy in places they like to holiday

- Buy in a place where they may like to retire

Does this sound familiar to you?

Although local knowledge is an important factor when buying real estate, this should not limit your options and restrict you to areas that you are familiar with.

You must never buy a property based on emotional reasons! If you wish to succeed with investing in property, you need to make logical decisions based on sound principles of real estate investing.

You can use different strategies in real estate to grow your portfolio. These include investing in rental apartments, single family homes, industrial property, retail real estate, office space, hospitality or overseas properties. You can also gain expertise in lease options, investing in off plan property or buying at foreclosure sale. But these can never replace the fundamental principles of real estate investing.

There can be various strategies but the principles of real estate investing are eternal.

There are many experienced investors who become overconfident and violate these principles—they invariably suffer grave consequences. So please take time to study the following fundamental principles of real estate investing with care.

'Buy and Hold' will Make You Rich

Always remember that you buy property for capital appreciation. Real estate first and foremost is a capital business. Rent and cash flow are important to help you own the property for long term.

"Don't wait to buy real estate, buy real estate and wait."

~Will Rogers (1935)

Investing means owning real estate for long term. Flipping properties and lease options strategies are used to generate cash to fund your long-term investments and should not be confused with the long-term goal of creating wealth through capital appreciation.

Real Estate is not a get-rich-quick scheme; capital appreciation happens over a period of time. You have to have patience, perseverance and persistence. For this, you have to understand the compounding power of real estate investing.

How many times investors have sold their property for peanuts only to realize a few years later that they would have made a fortune had they had the patience and wisdom to hold it a bit longer.

Please remember the times you have cursed your ancestors for selling a piece of real estate that would have changed your financial future and of the generations to come.

If you can help, never ever sell your property: this is one fundamental principle of real estate investing you should never forget.

'Cash flow' Funds Your Real Estate Business and Gives You Peace of Mind

When I started out in real estate, there were no books or real estate investment seminars. My mentor was a rustic real estate agent who gave me one great piece advice that has stuck in my mind for the past three decades. His advice was very straightforward: "*Only buy Cows that give milk.*" This one advice has kept me out of trouble in downturns in the property cycle and made me a successful investor.

It is cash flow that funds your lifestyle and gives you peace of mind. The happiest times of my life have been those when I was flush with money to pay my bills, take holidays and meet all my financial commitments. My worst nightmares came when I was low on cash flow to meet my mortgage requirements even when I owned millions of dollars' worth of real estate in my portfolio.

The main reasons why people get into trouble, have foreclosure sales and become bankrupt are that they fail to understand and monitor their cash flow.

You should subscribe to Warren Buffet's philosophy of investing for cash flow: whether you buy real estate or stocks ... buy only for cash flow. Capital gain will happen over a period of time with any good investment and cash flow, in the meantime, will help you fund your life style and keep you and your banks happy.

Never buy 'negatively geared' properties. A negatively geared property is a property wherein rent received from the tenant does not cover expenses related to the property such as mortgage payments, maintenance charges, rates, insurance, property management costs etc. There is no fun in buying properties that you will need to fund from your pocket on a monthly basis. There are many property gurus who will teach you to buy 'negatively geared' properties to avail tax refunds. This is plain and simple stupid—keeps away from such gurus.

How many properties can you buy if you have to keep supporting them from your hard earned money? What will happen if the interest rates go up, you lose your job or fall ill? Will you be able to continue supporting these properties? Always buy 'positively geared' properties that put cash into your pocket after paying all the expenses including mortgage payments.

Buy land only if you have adequate cash flow from other sources. Otherwise, stay away from land investments as they have little or no cash flow. Most people who got into trouble during the crash of 2008 - 2009 were investors with large land holdings or with negatively geared properties in their portfolios. When the market went down, they could not sell their properties even at a discount, resulting in mortgagee sales and bankruptcies. Stick with rental property investments that are cash cows and you will never go wrong.

Remember the good old saying, ***"Buy cows that give milk.***" This is the secret mantra to success in real estate and will keep you out of trouble when things go wrong.

Do the Math

Real estate investing has nothing to do with emotions. It is only numbers that matter. When you buy a house to live in, there are emotions involved: you have to have the comfort level, practicality and pride of ownership. Your house reflects your personality and provides security and warmth to your family.

Real estate investing is all about getting your numbers right. It is about yields on purchase price or market value and capitalization rates. You have to understand terms such as Market Value, Cash on Cash Return, Internal Rate of Return and Deposit Re-cycling Time. I have explained these terms at the end of the book (Refer Appendix). They may sound difficult at first, but are relatively easier to understand once you start applying them.

You have to take into account mortgage financing costs, out goings or cash deductions to work out pre-tax cash flows. And finally, you have to take into account the depreciation and other tax refunds to work out the after tax cash flow.

It is not humanly possible for anyone to work out these figures manually when you are comparing, let us say, five prospective properties to buy one. Fortunately, we have real estate investing software's and investment property calculators to help us in getting all the figures we need to make an invest decision.

If you concentrate on the numbers, it will be easier for you to **keep your emotions out** when buying an investment property.

To do the math is very important but you have to temper the mathematical outcome with subjective analysis and human judgment with regard to quality of construction, location, quality of the tenant and lease terms. You should never get carried away by numbers alone but subject them to your common sense judgment.

Location Location Location

If the location of your property is right you will never have problems in finding tenants. There is no point in buying a property that shows a great rate of return on paper but has high vacancy rates. Many investors fall prey to not taking into account the vacancy factor and get carried away in purchasing properties that show high yields.

The property you buy should be in the right demographic area where employment and population are on the rise. Once you have found the right geographic area focus further on neighborhoods that are close to places of employment, shopping centers, schools and transportation centers.

If the location is right, you will have capital growth because of demand.

People often question me, "If the location is so great, then the price of the property will increase because of a high demand and will pull down the rate of return, which will inevitably have an adverse impact on the cash flow from the property, won't it? Although there is some merit in this argument, astute investors will find ways and means to add value and increase cash flow by making improvements to the property.

Always Buy From a Motivated Seller

You make money in real estate when you buy. Even if you master the best skills, it is virtually impossible to sell a property above market value until and unless you find a really stupid buyer, which is rare. To make instant money in real estate, you have to buy below the market value, which can only be done through buying a property from a motivated seller. If a person has no motivation to sell then you will never be able to negotiate a great bargain price.

It is not unethical to buy property below its actual value. Selling at a low price becomes desirable when people wish to dispose of their property because of various reasons, which could be due to some urgent financial need. Property is an excellent investment but, at times, difficult to liquidate. You solve the vendor's problem by coming to their aid with immediate cash. If cash problems are not solved, banks can take over the property and they may lose everything.

There can be many reasons why vendors want urgent settlement and cash. Some of the reasons can be vendor going overseas on a lucrative assignment, divorce with couples wanting to separate move on with their lives, illness or death in a family requiring funds, business needs that require urgent injection of capital. While investing in real estate, you have to understand the vendor's problems and try and solve them in a way that it can work to the parties' advantage.

You can accumulate great wealth quickly by simply learning the art of finding motivated sellers and purchasing below market value. Supposing you buy a million dollar property for $900,000 – which is 10% below market value – if you are able to achieve that then you have created an instant wealth of $100,000.

Use Other People's Money (OPM) to Fund Your Real Estate

No one has ever become rich by using their personal money. Sooner than later, individuals and companies run out of money to fund their growth. You have to learn how to use Other People's Money or OPM to grow your net worth.

The business of banks is to use other people's money to make profits. They borrow from you and loan it to businesses at a higher interest rate to make money. You should think like a bank and borrow at reasonable cost of finance to fund your real estate business for much higher profits.

Real estate provides you with a great opportunity to use financial leverage to grow your wealth. Banks and other financial institutions love to finance real estate. The only way you can accelerate your growth is by using OPM and using financial leverage sensibly.

You have to insure that returns from the real estate investment are greater than the cost of borrowed funds.

Make Use of the Property Cycle

"Be fearful when others are greedy and be greedy only when others are fearful."

~Warren Buffett

Property Cycle, unlike stock prices, is very slow moving and comparatively easier to understand.

The easiest option for you is to buy real estate at the bottom of the cycle—but in real life, things are not so simple else everyone would be rich. The bottom of the property market is difficult to predict.

"Buy when everyone else is selling and hold until everyone else is buying.

This is not merely a catchy slogan. It's the very essence of successful investment."

~ J. Paul Getty (1976)

If you will wait for the property cycle to bottom out (which is hard to predict,) then you will be able to buy properties only once in seven to ten years and you will miss out on all the other opportunities that happen in other parts of the property cycle.

In real estate, you make money either through Cash flow, Capital Growth or Equity. These are known as the three corners of the property triangle. You will rarely be able to achieve all three at a particular stage in the property cycle. For instance, when the property prices are regressing, you cannot buy real estate for capital growth but it is an opportune time to buy properties below market value and create instant equity—which is better than waiting for capital growth. At the bottom of the cycle, you will be able to buy properties that give high cash flow as the prices are down and return on investment much better.

The beauty of property cycle is that it is very slow moving; you will get ample warning signs on things to come if you are not blinded by greed and emotions.

Negotiate Everything

If you are to be successful in real estate, you have to negotiate everything whether it is the price of the property, rent and lease terms with your tenants, mortgage rates with the banks, property management contracts or repairs, and upgradation costs with the traders.

Every time you negotiate, you save money and improve your chances of success. For example: by negotiating a 0.2% lower interest rate on a 30 year mortgage loan with your bank, you can save hundreds of thousands of dollars over the lifetime of the loan.

Everything in business is negotiable. If someone tells you otherwise, the person is a fool. Please stay away from him! Real estate negotiation is one skill that you have to master to become successful.

Learn to Walk Away from a Deal

Do not get emotionally attached to a deal. Learn to walk away if the numbers are not correct. The deal of a life time comes along every single day if you are on a constant lookout.

"The single most powerful tool for winning a negotiation is the ability to get up and walk away from the table without a deal."

Knowledge of Real Estate Investing is the Key to Success

Knowledge of real estate investing is the biggest leverage you can apply to succeed in real estate. Whether you are a newbie or an experienced property investor, you have to continuously upgrade your knowledge.

A brilliant investment property is never seen with the eyes but always with the mind. Thousands of people will pass a property and will see no any value in it. It takes an educated mind to understand what is the real value and potential of a property. At times, even vendors do not understand the full potential of their properties. Like everything in life, education is the key.

You have to constantly view deals, visit properties, read books, watch videos, attend seminars and, join property investor's forums regularly for fresh information; you have to acquire knowledge to an extent that it becomes your second nature. When you reach this stage, you will be able to spot a great real estate investing opportunity when you browse the internet, see an inconsequential advertisement in the newspaper or during your morning walk.

Buildings Depreciate, Land Appreciate

This is an extremely important principle to understand. Land appreciates over a period of time whereas buildings depreciate. The value of a property consists of land and improvements. Land generates very little or no cash flow; it is mostly the improvements or buildings on the property that generate cash flow.

Buy properties that have large land element whilst keeping an eye on cash flow.

Generally speaking, city apartments have higher rentals but little or no land element. Over a period of time, apartment buildings become old and dilapidated—they lose in value. Single family homes, on the other hand, have lesser cash flow due to the land element. The trick is to buy discounted properties from motivated sellers and increase the rental returns through improvements such as adding additional rooms or building an additional home on the vacant land if permitted by the council.

Even as buildings depreciate in value, the underlying increase in value of land will make you rich.

"Buy on the fringe and wait. Buy land near a growing city! Buy real estate when other people want to sell. Hold what you buy!"

~John Jacob Astor (1848)

Take Action

Taking action is the key to your success. There is no point in having all the knowledge and not applying towards your success.

It is fear that keeps people away from buying real estate. Knowledge – to some extent – abates this fear. However, no one can reach a state of complete knowledge to overcome fear. You have to act in good faith and intelligence; inaction will keep you tied to poverty. Once you start taking action, your experience and confidence in real estate investing will increase.

Action is always superior to inaction. When I started out, I had no knowledge of real estate investing. My mentor was a very rustic real estate agent. He pushed me hard into buying my first property probably because he wanted to make a commission. The only sensible thing I did was to take the leap of faith and get pushed into buying my first investment property. I have never looked back since. For the first few years, I was a 'street smart' real estate investor ... I was learning by taking action.

I never learnt anything new at a property seminar that was not in a book. What helped me was the synergy of like-minded people: it helped me overcome my fear of investing. If so many people could do it successfully, so could I. The best way to overcome fear and taking action is to find a mentor and join a group of successful real estate investors.

Take action even if you have limited knowledge about real estate investing. Think big but start small. A few small steps will change the outcome of your life.

Finance

Finance is the life blood of real estate. To be successful in real estate, you have to understand how to fund your property purchases with the least cost and risk involved. It is important to understand how the power of leverage works: proper leveraging can make your wealth grow exponentially and its improper use can make you bankrupt within a very short period of time.

It is also important to understand property tax laws and how a property investor, you can take advantage of those laws to fund your real estate purchases. The biggest expense in your lifetime is the taxes you pay to the government. If you are smart, you don't have to pay those taxes. Real estate investment gives you an opportunity to save on those taxes legally and fund your lifestyle from those savings. There are ways and means to structure your real estate investments not only to save on taxes but also to provide protection to your assets.

Understanding and applying these basic principles is the key to success in real estate investing.

REAL ESTATE INVESTMENT STRATEGIES

There are many exciting real estate strategies you can use to create massive wealth through real estate; you do not have to use all the strategies but master only a few. The investment strategy that is most suited to you will depend upon your investment plan.

Investment Plan

It is extremely important to have an investment plan!

A person who is starting out in real estate will have a totally different strategy as opposed to those who have experience and substantial funds to invest. For instance, if you are with no money and bad credit rating you, will need to improve your credit rating first, become a property finder for other investors, do quick deals to generate cash flow and build equity. Once you have some money, it is advisable to start with residential homes as they are easy to understand and rent.

On the other hand, if you are an investor with high income and tax problems you may look to buy to buy properties with high capital growth potential even though they have slightly lower cash flow. A high net worth investor will look at buying commercial buildings, shopping malls or overseas investment properties.

Your plan will be defined by the starting point of your journey and the final outcome you wish to achieve. If you do not know the starting and the final destination points, you will not be able define the investment strategy you need to follow.

Your starting point will be defined by your knowledge of real estate investing, the amount of capital and cash flow that you have. It will also depend on your risk taking profile and your age. If you are young, you will be able to take more risks but if you are older, you need to be more conservative.

The destination point will be defined by the scale of your ambition. Real estate strategy you use will also depend upon how fast or how slow you wish to reach your destination and what kind of time and effort you are willing to devote.

Investment Strategies

Some of the real estate investment strategies that you can use are enumerated below:

Property Assignment - In this investment strategy you negotiate and find a property deal. Get the property under contract and then pass it on to a real estate investor for a fee.

Contemporaneous Settlements - This is a property transaction in which you buy and sell property on the same day. If this investment strategy is applied correctly you can make a fantastic profit without having the need to settle or raise a mortgage.

Buy off the Plans - By using this investment strategy you benefit from the developers and buy property at a discount off the plans. Generally by the time property is constructed there will be some capital appreciation.

Delayed Settlement - By putting a property under contract and delaying settlement you get the advantage of capital growth when the market is moving up. Alternately you can use the time to make improvement to the property and increase its value.

Use Credit Cards to Purchase and Renovate Properties - This is a good investment strategy wherein you use zero interest money from credit cards to make the down payment and increase the value of your property through renovations. You then refinance the property to pay of the credit card debt before it becomes due.

Use Non Traditional Lenders - By raising capital from second tier lenders, private investors, equity partnerships, bridging finance you can pump up your profits dramatically.

Vendor Finance - By using this investment strategy you can buy No Money Down properties.

Negative Gearing - When this investment strategy is used correctly, it is like getting interest free loans from the Government in form of tax refunds. Negative gearing is advisable only for individuals who have very high cash flow and taxable incomes. I personally do not subscribe to this strategy, but it's important that I state it explicitly because as an investor, you will come across this terminology when developers are trying to sell overpriced properties.

Equity Release - This is another great investment strategy to use your equity to either buy more real estate or fund your life style. Better still the money is tax free cash.

Lease to Buy Options - There is a saying in real estate: *"it is not how much property you own that matters but how much property you control."* By using 'lease option investment strategy,' you can control a very large amount of real estate without actually buying it. In a lease option, you lease a property with option to buy at a later date when you have the money. By putting lease to buy option in your agreement, you control the property and capital appreciation will accrue to you when you buy.

Foreclosures - Many investors become experts at buying properties at foreclosures or mortgagee sales. By applying this investment strategy alone, you can become a very successful real estate investor.

This list is not comprehensive but only indicative.

Each real estate investment strategy has its place and can be used effectively to meet your stated goal in life. Which strategy you use at a particular point in time will depend upon your plans based on personal circumstances and the position of the property cycle. But whatever strategy you use, you should do it with a very clear objective; you should always have an exit strategy in place in case things don't go as per your plans.

You will need to define your investment goal clearly before embarking on a particular strategy.

Retirement Planning

There are various investment strategies aimed towards retirement planning. Many people buy property to generate passive income so that they can go into early retirement and live life of leisure.

Most people in order to supplement their income during retirement either do reverse mortgage or take out a fresh loan against their equity in the property. The problem with this strategy is that they increase their leverage on the property at a time when they should be reducing their leverage. During retirement most people do not have cash flow from income to support additional mortgage payments.

It is wiser for retirees to readjust their property portfolio for cash flow before retirement. I will discuss this at length with an example.

Example of Retirement Planning

Raj Babar migrated to New Zealand at the age of 50 years in April 2003 with $150,000. His plan was to retire with a passive income of $150,000 per annum through property investment at the age of 65 years.

He attended several property seminars (free & paid) to understand the property market in New Zealand – to get better grasp of the real estate environment he became a real estate consultant as he felt knowledge was the key to growing rich.

Raj debated whether to buy an investment property or a residential house for his family. Although his investment knowledge and instincts told him to buy an investment property first, he decided to buy a house for his family to provide emotional stability to his wife and children in a new country.

Finance was easy during the period and after purchasing the house with 20% deposit he was left with enough money to pay deposit for an investment property.

The first property he purchased was a brand-new leasehold flat in the heart of Auckland CBD that had a ground rent holiday for 7 years. Although he knew capital appreciation on the property will be low as compared to a freehold property, he bought the property for 12% net return ROI. He improved the cash flow to

14% by furnishing the flat with furniture, television, refrigerator and kitchen utensils – he did this in order to improve his position with the banks for future borrowing.

Raj's strategy was very simple: his aim was to buy freehold property with a minimum of 10% return … such properties did not exist in Auckland. The rate of return on investment (ROI) for a freehold single family home in Auckland, New Zealand at the time was 5–6%. This was well below his stated goal. So he focused on single family homes that had additional land to construct a second house.

Raj would scout hundreds of property to find a motivated seller who was willing to sell his property at least 10–20% below market value for immediate settlement, which would give an initial return of around 7% on his investment and also give him instant equity. To increase his rate of return, he made cosmetic improvements to the first house and construct a second house on the property without sub-dividing the property. This was because sub-division costs were around $60,000 and this expense would not add to his rate of return. The aim was not to sell the second house but to increase his return on investment.

The rent after construction of second house on the property normally increased his return to over 10%. The act of constructing the second house and improvements to the first house increased the valuation of the property by 20%. The fact that he bought the property below market valuation worked in his favor, and subsequent improvements increased his equity in the property by over 30%. He then used the additional equity to pay deposit to buy another investment property. Banks were happy to loan because cash flow from the existing properties added to Raj's income.

It took Raj around 6 months to complete one project. He repeated the process again and again as it was a winning formula.

Once a project was completed, he handed over management of the property to a competent property manager. From then on, it became a hands-off operation with residual cash flowing from it. His only work was to check receipt of rents every month and once in a while give decision on a major maintenance issue. There were times when he did not speak with his property manager for months or even a year. By increasing the return on investment to over 10%, he ensured that the property became not only self-supporting (pay for the all its expenses, mortgage and management costs,) but also gave him a small residual cash flow every week.

There are people who try and manage properties themselves and then cry foul about the headache of managing tenants. This is not residual or retirement income; Raj paid his property managers 6% of the gross rental but this is an expense. In effect he paid them only 4% because of tax rebate. His vacancy rates were much lower as compared to when he was managing his properties. He calculated that if his property manager could reduce vacancy by one week in a year, then there was zero cost of management. By appointing competent property managers several properties owned by Raj have not had one day of vacancy in over 7 years.

Finding a good property manager made Raj's income stream residual. Every property manager is not equal but with some experience, proper research and interviewing you can find property managers who will take all the headaches of property management from you—which is true for any business!

As a result of his property investment, Raj did not pay a single dollar tax on his income for the first 12 years. In later years, he was getting tax rebates to the tune of $35,000 per year. He used this money to fund additional property purchases.

Raj treats each property as a separate business center and an independent source of residual income stream. He repeated this simple formula several times over.

After years of successfully following this strategy, Raj had to change tack because of increase in Council fees and construction prices; nothing lasts forever. But for as long as it lasted, he managed to buy several properties that gave him residual income.

Raj then worked on a new strategy of finding large houses in key locations that could be converted into room by room rentals for young professionals. This provided him with even larger cash flows.

Using strategies outlined above, Raj bought $8.0 million worth of residential properties and built equity of $3.0m. He had built substantial residual income but it did not match up to his goal of $150,000 p.a. to retire. This was because of his liabilities of monthly mortgage payments and outgoings.

As part of his final strategy to retire, Raj sold all his residential investment properties and used the proceeds to buy unencumbered commercial properties worth $3.0 million giving 8% net return. The advantage of investing in commercial properties is that tenant pays all outgoings such as rates, insurance, body corporate fees and even the property management fees: he now has no borrowings and can enjoy his retirement in peace.

The story that I narrate is not work of fiction but based on true life story.

Residential Vs Commercial Real Estate Investing

It is important to understand differences between residential property investments as compared to investing in commercial real estate. They are completely different kettle of fish.

Complexity

Residential real estate investment, as the name suggests, is investing in property that people use primarily for residential accommodation. These include apartments, town houses, free-standing homes, duplexes, condominiums and apartment buildings.

Residential real estate investment is comparatively less daunting than commercial real estate when starting out your journey because everyone knows what constitutes a home that some could live in. You will straight away notice absence of a bathroom and a kitchen or if the property suffered from poor ventilation.

Commercial properties include offices, industrial sheds, free standing retail shop, bulk retail, block of shop, medical centers, service stations, motels, hotels, back packers, health clubs, churches, funeral parlors, child care centers, car yards, convenience stores, shopping malls, to name just a few. Each type of commercial real estate investment has its own peculiarities, strengths, problems, rewards and risks.

In addition, you have to deal with contracts and leases that can affect the price of the property.

Commercial real estate investment is the natural progression from residential property investment. Experienced property investors tend to move into commercial real estate sooner than later – and for very good reasons.

Once your portfolio grows, it is very difficult to manage your investments if a large portion of them is tied in residential properties. Imagine you have $15 million worth of residential properties – that would be lot of homes and tenants to take care of.

On the other hand, $15 million will buy only a very small number of commercial properties, which will be comparatively easier to manage with much lesser overheads.

Tenants

In residential real estate investment, you are essentially dealing with people. Unfortunately, people create problems. Your tenant will ring you up at all odd times with even the smallest of complaints: at times the rent is not paid in time, the lawns are not mowed or they will not keep the property clean and in worst cases, they damage your property.

Residential tenants have little or no interest in maintaining your property.

"The working components of a rental home (heating, cooling, electrical, plumbing, dishwasher, garbage disposal, doorbell and refrigerator) will break down 90% faster on the rental than the working components of your own home."

If the tenant is not complaining, then you will find the neighbor complaining about the tenant for making too much noise or their children running into the neighbor's property. So, you need people skills to manage your property or you will need to employ a property manager.

"The sweet little girl with the baby you rented your house to will always have an abusive boyfriend, and their loud, passionate lovemaking at night, nasty quarrels and scream fests will be the talk of the neighborhood."

If you have ever worked as a landlord—this reason will be very clear to you: residential tenants complain about everything on earth and mostly in the middle of the night or when you are watching a good game of football.

Commercial property on the other hand, is a space for doing business. It is a place from where a tenant sells his products and services. The success of his business depends on the presentation of the property and number of visitors they receive each day.

The tenant bases his monthly rent on a commercial property on a certain percentage of the profit the business makes each month. When a businessman approaches you to rent a property, they do so because the location is suitable to them.

The tenants know the value of a good location and they will pay to be in the right place.

Most commercial property tenants will fix problems and carry out minor repairs on their own without calling the landlord. This is because they realize that problems need to be taken care of immediately or they will interfere with their business. Residential tenants on the other hand, will always look for help from the landlord to take care of repairs—they will never spend a dime on the property.

Commercial property tenants can spend substantial money to upgrade the property for their business requirement. These improvements stay with the property long after the tenant has moved on.

Most commercial tenants need to put in networking and cable wires, sound systems, and electrical outlets – all of which increase the market value and marketability of your commercial property.

In commercial property, you tend to deal with contracts where as in residential real estate investment you tend to deal with people.

Vacancy Rate

The biggest advantage of residential real estate investment is that it is fairly easy to find a new tenant once your property becomes vacant, which reduces the vacancy rate and there is always cash flow coming from your investment.

There is only one reason for your property to remain vacant for too long: your rents are too high for that location at the particular time. If you drop the rent by 5–10%, you will normally find a tenant, which is because people have to live somewhere at affordable costs.

In commercial real estate, properties are far more specialized and in case of a vacancy, you may not find a tenant for months or even a few years: this is a huge risk for a new investor who is not familiar with real estate investment and requires deeper pockets in case of vacancy.

Rate of Return

The return on investment in commercial real estate is much higher than residential property: the income is net and not gross because the tenant pays all the outgoing expenses and is also more stable because of the long leases.

The rate of return on residential real estate investment is much lower because in residential property, the owner has to pay all the outgoing expenses such as property rates, insurance, body corporate fees and maintenance costs. In commercial real estate, it is the responsibility of the tenant to pay these costs thereby increasing net returns.

It is typical to have returns of around 7–10% net for a commercial real estate investment and anywhere from 5–7% net return for a prime property.

The net return from residential property tends to be from 2–6% and can be a bit higher in less desirable neighborhoods and apartment buildings.

Value of Property

The value of a property is determined by its location, land size and improvements. This is true for both residential and commercial property.

What is peculiar to commercial real estate is that its value is also greatly determined by the quality of the lease. In general, the value is determined by taking net contractual rental being paid and use of a capitalization rate to arrive at a value. The value is also determined by the quality of the tenant and length of the lease.

There is a saying in commercial real estate: ***"More leases you read in bed the richer you will become."***

The value of a commercial property can drop substantially if it becomes vacant. Often commercial properties are sold at 10–50% of their value if they are difficult to lease.

The value of residential real estate on the other hand, is determined to a large extent by location of the property. If the house is in a desirable area, it will command a better price.

Property leases

Residential property leases tend to be very short when compared to commercial leases that can run for several years. As discussed earlier, it is much easier to find a tenant for vacant residential property.

Finance

The funding for commercial real estate investments is harder to get as banks look at the quality of tenants, length and terms of lease.

In general, commercial properties are more expensive than residential properties. Banks will lend up to 90 % or more on residential properties and only up to 50% to 70% on commercial property. You will therefore need more equity to buy. This reduces your leveraging power to buy more property

The lending rates are also marginally higher, which reflects the risk that banks associate with commercial real estate investment.

You will require much lesser seed capital to start with residential real estate investment and will be able to leverage your money better with residential property.

Government Laws

Government laws with respect to residential property are far more stringent and can override anything that you may have written in the rental agreement with the tenant. Politicians and bureaucrats put these protections in place so that residential tenants are not exploited.

In some countries and states the laws are so much in favor of the tenant that you cannot evict them even in case they are behind on their rents.

Real estate law is more flexible towards commercial lease contracts. You can insert any clauses in the sale or lease agreement that is agreeable to the contracted parties without any interference from the governing agencies.

It is common to charge penalty interest on the outstanding rent or lock the premises on continued default of rent.

Property Management Costs

Residential real estate investment management takes time and effort because you deal with people. Once you have several residential investments, it can become a full-time job.

Residential property managers' charge anywhere from 6–8% of the rent collected towards the management fee.

Commercial properties on the other hand, do not require much of your time in managing them. Commercial tenants usually stay in the property for many years and it is in their best interest to maintain and make improvements to the property.

Commercial property management is also much simpler because tenants have a strong vested interest to maintain the property to a high standard: they usually derive their income from the property. They have to keep the property looking good and maintain functionality to impress their clients.

Commercial tenants spend hundreds of thousands of dollars to make improvements to the property. Most of these improvements stay with the property long after the tenant has left the property.

Commercial property management fees reflect the reduced work involved and charges range from 2–6% of the rent collected. The best part is that you can charge the management cost to tenant as a part of the out goings. In case you choose to manage the property then the management charges become payable to you thereby increasing the return from the property.

Risks and Rewards

So far, the biggest risk in commercial real estate investment is finding a new tenant in case of a vacancy. In commercial real estate, the requirement of each tenant in terms of size, location, use and rent payment capacity is so different that it is very difficult to get the right tenant for the right property.

For the reasons mentioned above, it is also difficult to sell or lease a commercial real estate investment. Generally speaking higher the value of property will result in lesser number of investors to buy the property.

A commercial real estate investment is less liquid than other investments because there are very few players in the market. For a residential house, there will be hundreds of potential buyers, which is not the case with commercial properties.

Commercial real estate investments are generally sold on capitalization rates and rarely on replacement value. It is therefore possible to purchase a poorly rented commercial property well below its market value. You can also increase the value of your commercial real estate simply by leasing the property or raising the rents during rent reviews or renegotiating the lease terms when it come up for renewal.

Commercial real estate investment provides professional investors higher returns and ease of managing them. For these investors, commercial property is their 'bread and butter' and they drive their speculative income by trading in residential properties.

Some commercial investors focus their attention to improve and add value to their commercial portfolio. Whilst others use their rental returns to fund development projects that show much higher returns, they need different and more advanced skill sets.

Commercial real estate investing is very rewarding but requires more knowledge, experience and capital out lay. It is not advisable to jump into commercial real estate from the very out set until and unless you have very deep pockets and risk-taking ability. It is advisable to start with residential real estate investment to build your equity and cash flow.

You should buy at least 8–10 residential property investments before venturing into the world of commercial real estate investment that is far more complex.

For a new investor, it is much easier and less risky to get started with residential real estate investing because of the easy in understanding residential property, getting the finances, leveraging money and managing vacancies.

REAL ESTATE FINANCE

Understanding real estate finance is the key to your success. As stated earlier, finance is the life blood of real estate: without finance there is no real estate.

"Empty pockets never held anyone back. Only empty heads and empty hearts can do that." -Dr. Norman Vincent Peale

It is critical for you to understand how to finance investment property if you are to be successful with your real estate investment business. A generation ago, the only viable option for most people was to get a loan from a bank. Today, you can get mortgage finance from myriads of banks, financial institutions, lawyers' client funds, real estate companies, building societies, insurance companies, credit unions, contributory mortgage companies or even the vendors.

Contrary to what people might have told you, banks want to loan you money. It is their business to loan money to make money. It is also equally important for an investor to use Other People's Money to leverage.

Banks and financial institutions that provide real estate finance look at your cash flow, equity position, credit rating and soundness of your real estate or property that you wish to buy.

Banks can be conservative with their money because the bank's risk is greater than yours as they loan you anywhere from 50–100% on the market value of the property. They don't even have direct control over the asset once the loan is given; they try to protect themselves with various clauses in the mortgage document. You have to understand these clauses in the loan agreement before you sign it.

You have to be sensitive to banks advice and concerns—they are your partners in business. You have to prepare to meet their lending criteria rather than attempting to fool them by hiding or furnishing wrong information. You will damage your long-term interest if you try and take short cuts. No bank will provide you with real estate finance if your credit rating or the reputation in the market suffers.

You have to organize your personal finances, improve your credit rating, prepare your financial information and that of the property that you wish to buy before approaching the bank for real estate finance. If you do not do your homework, lack confidence and don't present yourself properly then, no bank or financial institution will give a loan.

It is important to understand that the lending criterion of banks change from time to time. They may reject your application for a loan even if your finances are in great shape – this is because the lending criteria for a particular type of property you wish to buy may not match the lending criteria of the bank for that property. In such a situation, it is wiser to approach another bank for a loan. It is better to utilize the services of a competent mortgage broker who is well informed regarding the lending policies of various banks and will guide you to the most suitable lender.

You should shop around for the best interest rates. Believe it or not, interest rates are negotiable! It is a good idea to compare the interest rates of various lenders so you can negotiate with a lender of your choice. At times, interest rates can differ between different branches of the same bank. You can save from tens to hundreds of thousands of dollars during the life time of a loan by simply doing some research and negotiating hard.

Your profits and success will increase when you get a better grasp of various real estate finance strategies such as: revolving credit, vendor finance option, credit cards, private investor funding, using second mortgages, partnerships and joint ventures, refinancing and recycling your deposit.

You have to also understand the various types of mortgages available in the market to make use of them to your advantage. These include fixed and floating rates, interest only loans, capital repayment loans, reverse mortgages, split loans to name a few.

Understanding real estate finance is the key to your success. You have to understand how to get high on OPM. The secret is to find the best and cheapest source of funding of your property with least strings attached.

Strategy to Buy Outstanding Investment Properties

Once you have your finance approved, the next crucial question is how to buy investment property. If you are newbie, start with residential investment property because it is less risky and easy to understand.

The first property you buy is the most crucial—you cannot afford to make a mistake with your first buy. Once you have cash flow from several investment properties then a mistake in purchasing a wrong investment can be covered up. If something goes wrong with your first investment, it will set you back by several years before you can recover. It may also dent your confidence.

Some of the important criterion for selecting the right investment property is:

Area to Buy

Your first step involves buying an existing property in an area you understand (in your neighborhood) at or below market value. Buying below value will require some education and experience – this should not deter you because you have to start somewhere. So, this is the right time to start.

The property should be close to the area you live in. There is no point in buying properties that are 6 to 7 hours' drive away. You will waste your energy in commuting rather than renovating your property and increasing its value.

Try and buy property in a high capital growth area if possible. As investors, we make money through capital gain. However, cash flow is the key. Cash flow from property should support your investment purchases so that you can pay for all the outgoings without any stress. Also keep in mind interest rates as they may change in the future – check how they will impact your investment.

If you look around, you will find great investment opportunities in your neighborhood. The numbers have to stack up. Take all expenses into account. Amateurs at times over look certain expenses when carrying out calculations due to their optimism and excitement.

Once you start viewing and analyzing large number of deals, your mind will open to some of the finer points of investing.

Buying and Renovating

Buy a property that is structurally sound but in need of minor cosmetic repairs. You will be amazed how much value you can add to a property by doing some simple and inexpensive cosmetic changes. These can involve trimming the over grown garden, mowing the lawn, replace some light fittings, polishing the floorboards or changing the carpets, painting the walls or by simply removing the rubbish you can increase the value of the property by thousands of dollars.

Adding Value to a Property

You can add value to any property by making improvements but it should make financial sense. Each dollar you spend on improvements must add value by two to five times otherwise your effort is a waste of your resources.

Be very cautious of over capitalizing. If houses in a street are selling for, let us say $500,000 then even if you spend an exorbitant amount of money in renovations, you will never be able to increase its value over half a million. On the contrary, it makes sense to buy over capitalized properties even at market price especially when you wish to reside in them. Most people forget how much money they have sent over long periods in improving their properties.

You necessarily do not have to spend huge amounts of money in improvements to add value to a property – never ever buy a property that has structural problems! You can spend tens of thousands of dollars in corrections but they will not add a cent to value of your property. The only time you buy a property with structural issues is if it is being sold for a massive discount and you have the exact numbers on what it will cost you to get the repairs done. Once you open the Pandora's Box, you will be astonished by what you will find.

Some other strategies include:

- **Change of Zoning** –Purchasing property in an area where zoning is likely to change can enhance its value without spending a dime: change in number of units permitted on size of land, improving height restrictions, and conversion of land usage from farm to residential or residential to commercial all play a part.

- **Change of Use** – You can apply to Council for change of use of property. One such example is conversion of residential property to a boarding house. Recently, one of my clients purchased an old Church and converted it into a childcare center and soon after the conversion; he sold the property at thrice the purchase price.

- **Sub-Division** – You can buy a large piece of land then sub-divide it into small parcels and sell them at a huge profit.

- **Unit Titles** – You can buy multiple flats or units on a single certificate of title and then apply to council for individually unit titling them will greatly enhance the value.

- **Development in the area** – Buying properties in area with knowledge of future developments can greatly add value to your purchases. These can include roads, trains, schools, new factories that will generate employment, shopping malls, golf courses, clubs etc.

- **Buying a vacant commercial building and leasing it will increase its value**

- **Renegotiating lease terms and increasing rents** – You can buy under rented properties and then negotiate with tenants to increase rents to market will greatly improve your cash flow and increase value of the property.

Adding value means having knowledge that not many people have garnered. Most real estate agents – who are basically sales people – will not be able to guide you. This is something you, as an investor, have to develop through reading, investigation and awareness in the market place.

Someone right said: ***"The best property you have to invest in is that What Is In Between your two ears."***

It is specialized knowledge that separates winners from losers or men from boys. Once you attain sensitivity towards property, you will be able to visualize value that an untrained mind cannot see.

Renting

"Landlords grow rich in their sleep" John Stewart Mill

The basic principle of investing is that your tenants must pay your mortgage. You have to get your numbers right when buying an investment property; the rent must cover not only your mortgage but also the out goings such as rates, body corporate, insurance and maintenance. In some high capital growth areas rents may not cover the expenses. In such cases, you will need to cover the short fall from your salary or cash flow from business.

You must check the rents and vacancy rates in the area before buying a property. The property must be in an area close to schools, markets, communication centers, job centers, where there is large demand by tenants. There is no point in buying a property showing a very high return on investment but in an isolated area that is difficult to rent. Vacancy will reduce your return on investment.

Repeat the Process

The quickest process to grow your portfolio quickly is to learn the art of buying property below value. Then add value to the property by carrying out cosmetic renovations. For every dollar you spend on the property the value must go up by at least three to five times. You must then get your property revalued. The extra equity that you create can be used as deposit for your next purchase.

The faster you repeat this process; faster will your net worth grow. This is called the 'Deposit Recycling Time' which means how fast you can get your initial deposit out of your investment property and use it as deposit to buy another property. Do not get lured into projects that show huge profit but will take very long time to complete or are risky in nature. Keep it simple and quick. Sorter your deposit recycling time the richer you will become.

Cash flow

A word of caution: you must always keep a tab on your cash flow. Most people do not comprehend the importance of cash flow and get into trouble. Most mortgagee sales and foreclosure take place because people under estimate the importance of cash flow.

When you're starting out, buy only cash flow positive properties – do not buy negatively geared properties (that take money out of your pocket.) Banks will lend you if you have both cash flow and equity; you will need to balance both these aspects if you are to become a successful property investor.

How to Find Good Investment Properties?

The next obvious question is: how to find the perfect property?

Which is the best place to start? Without doubt, your search should start with the internet. The internet will save you hours and hours of your time and effort.

The old theory on how to buy investment property will tell you to visit 100 properties, short list 30, make offer on 10 of them, get vendor response on three of them and finally buy one does not work in this fast-paced world. You will lose interest after viewing 5 properties because of the leg work involved.

The internet has changed how you find good investment properties. There is so much data available on the internet, not only regarding properties for sale in your area of interest but also recent sales, council rates, rental rates, vacancy rates, mortgage rates etc. that you can check the numbers on your investment if they meet your buying criteria before rushing to view the property.

You must sign up for a popular internet real estate site in your area; most sites will give you an option to search by price range, location, number of bedrooms and key search terms.

In your preferred area and price range (depending upon your finance approval) look for properties that have maximum number of bedrooms and land area. Number of bedrooms will decide how much rent you will get from the property. A four-bedroom house will normally command a better rent than a three-bedroom house. So, in your budget, try and buy a house that has maximum number of bedrooms. A large land area will give you options for the future. Always remember buildings depreciate whereas land appreciates in value.

By entering words like 'motivated vendor', 'diseased estate', 'mortgagee sale', 'urgent sale' etc. in the search criteria, you can short list properties that are likely to be sold below value.

Once you have short listed the properties, don't rush to view them – save fuel! It is very expensive and you will also save the environment. You must now speak with the real estate agents of the short-listed properties on phone to find out about the condition of the house, construction materials, likely rent, vacancy rates in the area, government and market valuation, location of the house in relationship to the land, proximity to schools, public transport, other amenities and as to why is the vendor selling the property.

Try and collect all the facts and financial figures like land rates, body corporate expenses, insurance rates etc. You must feed these figures into a property investment software (you can choose from many software's available in the market depending upon your budget) to arrive at gross return, net return after tax, IRR and cash flow. Buying an investment calculator is a small investment that is absolutely necessary and will help you compare various options available to you.

Only once you are satisfied with the quality of property, numbers and financial returns should you fix up a time to view the property.

The above process should not lull you into becoming an armchair investor. There is no better way to get the feel of an area without viewing several properties. Attend as many open homes you can and talk to various people like your accountant, lawyer, real estate agents and other property investors. This is especially more important when you are starting out.

Another important fact you must remember is that most good investment properties sell before they are advertised in the newspaper or come on the internet. You have to befriend few real estate agents in the area where you wish to buy the property and tell them of your requirements. Other sources of information can be lawyers, mortgage brokers, accountants and bank managers.

Real estate agents love to work with professional real estate investors because they get repeat sales. It is very important that you give them due respect and not waste their time. A good real estate agent will inform you regarding properties that are not even listed and are likely to come to the market shortly. You can do your due diligence on these properties and react before anyone else does with cash offers.

Remember that there is no perfect investment property—it is always a trade-off. If it is high cash flow, the capital-gain prospect may be low. If there is more land for future development, then the initial cash flow may not be as per your expectation. If the price is low, there may be additional costs involved in doing up the property before it can be leased. The property you buy will depend upon your situation and long-term plan.

Buying investment property can be a very simple and an enjoyable process if you follow the fundamentals correctly.

Formulas to Assess Value of an Investment Property

Want to assess the commercial real estate value quickly? You can assess the property value of a commercial building very simply by applying the three under-mentioned formulas. You can use these values to decide whether you wish to proceed ahead with the deal being offered.

Assess Value by Comparing Net Rent on the Building to Market Rent

Arrive at the net rent on the property by subtracting all the non-recoverable outgoings from the gross rent that the tenant is paying. Divide the net rental with net lettable area to arrive at rent per square meter. Compare the rent per square meter of the building with the market rent per square meter that is being achieved by similar properties. By comparing the two figures you will know if the property is under rented or over rented or at market rent.

Always try to buy a building that is under rented because there will be rental growth. The simplest way to increase the commercial real estate value of a building is by increasing the rents during reviews.

Compare Value by Applying the Capitalization Rate

Check from property valuers, real estate agents, banks, solicitors and recent sales what are the cap rates for similar types of building in the area. Determining cap rates is bit of a subjective judgment as they keep changing depending upon the market conditions and interest rates.

You divide the net rent from the property by the cap rate to determine the market value of the property. Compare the derived commercial real estate value with the price being asked by the vendors. By this simple calculation you will know if the asking price is below or more than the market value.

Compare the Land and Building Cost

You can calculate land and building cost by simply dividing the asking price with the building area of the property that you are buying. For example if the asking price is $2 million for a 1000 m2 commercial building. Then by dividing the asking price of $2 million by 1000 m2 we will get a land and building cost of $2000 per square meter.

By comparing the land and building cost with construction cost of a new building including price of land you will know how the property you intend to buy compares with the replacement cost. If there is a reasonable gap in the land and building costs and if the building compares favorably with the new building then you will have an opportunity to increase the rents and improve the commercial real estate value of the property.

Capitalization rates (or cap rates) is a factor used to determine the market value of commercial property for a known net rental.

It provides a comparative measure for investors to roughly estimate market value a property based on its income. It reflects the yield on a property which is another word for return on investment.

The formula for Cap rate is:

Cap rate(%) = Net Annual Rent / Value of Property

A more useful derivation of the formula above is used to determine the value of a property based on a Cap rate:

Value of Property = Net Annual Rent / Cap rate(%)

For example if the net rent from a property is $100,000 and the prevailing cap rate for this type of the building in the area is 10% then the value of the property will be:

Value of Property = $100,000 / 0.1 = $1,000,000.00

As an investor you have to have very clear understanding about the relation between property value and capitalization rate.

As the Cap rate increases the value goes down and when the Cap rate decreases the value goes up.

Real Estate Investment Advisers

The quality of real estate investment advisers that you choose to work with will define your success. The people who are most like to advise you on property matters are real estate agents, property valuers, lawyers, and accountants. You may also like to consult your bank manager, property manager, trades people, builder and architect.

These real estate investment advisers will form your core team that will define your success. Inputs from them will affect the quality of decision you make. Therefore it is important for you to surround yourself with the best possible team.

Always remember that you approach your team for advice only. You should never let them make decisions for you. Also remember that each member of your team is an independent contractor with his own agenda. For instance a solicitor will normally guide you towards caution as he does not wish his advice to have any adverse impact at a later date. An accountant will only look at the numbers and not the property and its future potential. A real estate agent may highlight only the positives and not the downside of the property.

Ask questions, listen to everybody but keep your council. Final decision is always your responsibility. You will need to weigh the pros and cons, take into account risks and returns before making a final decision.

Real estate investment advisers that you select should invariably be property investors themselves. If they are property investors their quality of advice will be much superior because they will have a much deeper insight.

When you are starting out don't get intimidated by the professionals you meet specially the ones who wear suits and sit in flashy offices. They may confuse you with their jargon and knowledge and may make you feel inadequate. It is important to remember that these real estate investment advisers are there to do a job for you for which you are paying them. If you don't understand something ask them to explain it to you in layman terms.

Beware of people who call themselves experts. There are bankers who dish out millions of dollars in property loans but don't own a single investment property. Same is true for some smooth talking real estate agents, accountants and solicitors who will give you advise without any worthwhile investments in their portfolio.

If you wish to seek advice go to people who have been there before you. Advice from such people is priceless and will save you hundreds and thousands of dollars.

Ask questions and do some background checks before employing services of a professional as a member of your team.

In many ways you will only be as good as your team of real estate investment advisors. Do not hesitate to pay a few extra dollars to hire the services of the best professional. Your investment in your team will pay you hundred times over.

Conclusion

I will conclude this book with the great words of wisdom written by an unknown writer on land. I hope and pray that they leave a deep imprint on your mind.

Who Am I?

I am the basis of all wealth, the heritage of the wise, the thrifty and prudent.

I am the poor person's joy and comfort, the rich person's prize, the right hand of capital,

The silent partner of thousands of successful people.

I am the solace of the widow, the comfort of old age, the cornerstone of security against misfortune and want.

I am handed down through generations, as a possession of great value.

I am the choicest fruit of labor, the safest collateral and yet I am humble.

I stand before every person bidding them to know me for what I am and asking them to possess me.

I am quietly growing in value through countless days.

Though, I might seem dormant, my worth increases, never failing, never ceasing.

Time is my aid and the ever-increasing population adds to my gain. I defy fire and the elements, for they cannot destroy me.

My possessors learn to believe in me and invariable they become envied by those that have passed me by.

While all other things wither and decay, I alone survive.

The centuries find me younger, always increasing in strength.

All oil and minerals come from me.

I am the producer of food, building materials and the home to every living thing.

I serve as the foundation for homes, factories, banks and stores.

I have not been produced for millions of years, yet, I am so common that thousands,

Unthinking and unknowingly, pass me by.

Who am I? "I AM Land."

My only addition to the wonderful thoughts of this writer is: buy land with improvements on it so that there is adequate cash flow to put some money in your pocket after expenses.

The purpose of this book will be served if it helps in educating and help morph enlightened people who create wealth the right way, preserve wealth the right way and ultimately, use their wealth for the greater good of humanity. This process leads to seeking a higher purpose in life and its fulfillment. I hope and pray that to some extent, that purpose is served. If you have read to this point, I thank you with gratitude in my heart and hope you succeed in creating true wealth that helps not only you and your family but entire humanity.

If you liked the book and gained some knowledge that will be useful to you in life, then please leave an honest review to help others find this book. It will be a small effort on your part, but an act of charity that may help in changing few lives for the better. I thank you in advance for your help.

This book is about fundamental principles of wealth creation through investing in properties. At Wealth Creation Academy, we teach multitude ways to generate passive income, which includes: real estate investing, digital publishing, affiliate marketing, multi-level marketing and investing in forex, commodities, and shares by copying experienced traders that need very little of time. You may like to get started with some of the strategies depending on your budget and time.

Other Books by the Author

Praveen Kumar has authored several bestselling books. Please visit his website http://praveenkumarauthor.com/ for more information

About the Authors

Praveen Kumar was abandoned by his father at the age of fourteen and joined the Navy at tender age of fifteen where education, roof and free food were guaranteed.

In order to understand the root cause of suffering he turned towards philosophy and religion. After 10 years of soul searching and meditation he understood that 'life is 'and material and spiritual world are closely interwoven. You cannot live in one without the other.

Praveen was highly successful in the Navy, where he successfully commanded submarines, sailed around the world in a yacht and received gallantry award for his contribution to the Navy.

Despite his success in the Navy, Praveen realized that lack of financial security for his family was one of key root causes of his suffering, resulting from his childhood deprivation. To improve his financial standing, Praveen took pre-mature retirement from the Navy to build his financial future through investing in Real Estate. The decision to educate on financial matters paid off, and today he and his wife are comfortably retired on six-figure passive income.

His aim is to help others create wealth in an enlightened way and empower them to live a healthy and happy life. He dedicates his time to write books and articles on financial and spiritual matters.

Prashant graduated with distinction from Auckland University as a computer engineer and later completed his MBA from the world's leading institution - INSEAD. During his successful corporate career, he worked for the most reputable consulting firms in the world - BCG & Deloitte - and represented New Zealand on Prime Minister-led trade missions to South East Asian countries.

After successfully generating income through his passive investments in property and stocks, Prashant decided to team up with his father to help people transform their lives through the leverage of financial education.

Their website http://wealth-creation-academy.com/ is devoted to teaching people how to create Multiple Streams of Passive Income through investing in real estate, online marketing and creating digital products.

Appendix

Real Estate Formulas

To be successful in real estate, it is important to understand the math and finance behind investing. This includes knowledge of formulas and ratios. These may look complex at first but are relatively easier to understand and master. The good news is that there are investment calculators that will do the grunt work and give all projections for sound decision making. Calculations apart you still need to understand what each terminology means to know the value and returns of an investment.

Gross Scheduled Income (GSI)

Gross Scheduled Income is the rental income collected in a year assuming the property is 100% tenanted and all rents are collected. Rents of vacant units are included at their reasonable market rent for the purpose of calculation.

Gross Scheduled Income = Rental Income (actual) + Vacant Units (at market rent)

Gross Operating Income (GOI)

Gross Operating Income (GOI) is calculated after subtracting from the GSI income from vacancies and adding income derived from other sources such as coin-operated laundry facilities. GOI can be considered as actual income the investor collects from the rental property.

Gross Operating Income = Gross Scheduled Income - Vacancy and Credit Loss + Other Income

Operating Expenses (OPEX)

OPEX function on annual costs associated with keeping a property in service and fully operational. These include body corporate fees, property taxes, insurance, routine maintenance and payment of utilities. Payments made for mortgages, capital expenditures or income taxes are not included in OPEX.

Net Operating Income (NOI)

Net Operating Income is arrived after subtracting OPEX from the Gross Operating Income.

Net Operating Income = Gross Operating Income - Operating Expenses

NOI is an important indicator to a property investor to arrive at a price he is willing to pay for an income stream. It determines the property's market value.

Cash flow before Tax (CFBT)

Cash flow before Tax is the income a property generates in a given year before tax after deducting all expenses.

Cash flow before Tax = Net Operating Income - Debt Service

Cap Rate

Cap Rate or Capitalization Rate is the ratio between the net operating income and a property's market value. It is a very popular term used to calculate a property's estimate of market value.

Cap Rate = Net Operating Income ÷ Market Value

Or,

Market Value = Net Operating Income ÷ Cap rate

Note of Caution – You can arrive at totally different and wrong market value by applying wrong Cap Rate. Great effort should be taken to find out the correct Cap Rate for a particular type of property in a given area.

Cash on Cash Return (CoC)

Cash-on-cash return is used in real estate to calculate the cash income earned vis-a-vis cash invested in a property.

Cash on Cash Return = Cash flow Before Taxes ÷ Initial Capital Investment

Most investors usually look at cash-on-cash as it relates to cash flow before taxes during the first year of ownership.

Calculating the Cash-On-Cash Return

For example, a real estate investor invests in an industrial warehouse that does not produce monthly income. Let us say the total purchase price of the property is $1 million. The investor puts 10% ($100,000) down and borrows $900,000 from the bank. In the first year, the investor pays maintenance and insurance costs of $10,000 out of pocket.

In the first year, the investor pays $25,000 in loan payments which includes $5,000 is principal repayment and $20,000 towards interest. This will imply that the investor's total out of pocket cash outflow during the first year is $135,000

After one year, the investor sells the property for $1.1 million. After repaying debt owed to the bank of $895,000, he is left with a cash inflow of $205,000.

In this case, the investor's cash-on-cash return is: ($205,000 - $135,000) / $135,000 = 51.9%. This is a very healthy return in one year. In case the property was rented, CoC would have been higher.

Cash-on-Cash return can also be used to forecast future cash earnings from an investment. It is an estimate of what an investor may expect to receive over the life of the investment.

Operating Expense Ratio (OER)

Operating Expense Ratio is the ratio between a real estate investment's total operating expenses dollar amount to its gross operating income. It is expressed as a percentage.

Operating Expense Ratio = Operating Expenses ÷ Gross Operating Income

Higher OER is matter concern when a commercial property is vacant. The owner will need to pay OPEX out of pocket that can considerably bring down rate of return from a property.

Debt Coverage Ratio (DCR)

Debt Coverage Ratio (DCR) is the ratio between annual net operating income and debt service (includes both principal and interest loan payments.)

Debt Coverage Ratio = Net Operating Income ÷ Debt Service

What DCR ratios indicate?

- Less than 1.0 – Net Operating Income will not cover debt servicing requirement.

- Exactly 1.0 – Net Operating Income will just about cover the debt requirement.

- Greater than 1.0 – There is adequate Net Operating Income to cover the debt

Break-Even Ratio (BER)

Lenders use BER to calculate ratio between the cash out flow to cash inflow from a property to determine how vulnerable the investment is to defaulting on its debt obligations. BER is expressed as percent.

Break-Even Ratio = (Operating Expense + Debt Service) ÷ Gross Operating Income

BER analysis:

- Less than 100% - expenses are less than income. Investment is in healthy shape.

- Greater than 100% - expenses are more than income being generated. This is matter of concern to lenders as the investor may default in case they do not have alternate sources of cash flow.

Loan to Value (LTV) or Loan to Value Ratio (LVR)

Loan to Value is the ratio between the loan amount to property's selling price or appraised value (whichever is lesser.) LVR is the lending criteria that financial instructions apply when approving a loan. It depends on their policy and type of property against which the loan is being given. LTV determines the leverage that an investor can use when purchasing an investment property. A higher leverage can result in higher returns but can also be risky.

Loan to Value = Loan Amount ÷ Lesser of Selling Price or Appraised Value

Annual Depreciation Allowance

Annual depreciation allowance is the annual tax deductions allowed on an investment property. It varies depending upon the tax code of a country.

Depreciable Basis = Property Value x Percent Allotted to Improvements

Next step:

Annual Depreciation Allowance = Depreciable Basis ÷ Useful Life

Taxable Income

Taxable income is the amount which the owner has to pay based on taxable income derived from the property which is calculated as per the formula below:

Taxable Income = Net Operating Income - Mortgage Interest – Depreciation - Capital Additions - Closing Costs + plus Interest earned in bank or escrow

To arrive at the tax payable by an investor, Taxable Income is multiplied by marginal tax rate.

Tax Liability = Taxable Income x Marginal Tax Rate

Cash flow after Tax (CFAT)

Cash flow after Tax. as the name suggests, is the cash flow accruing from a property after paying tax.

Cash flow after Tax = Cash flow before Tax - Tax Liability

This is the money that an investor can spend to either support their lifestyle or to make future purchases.

Time Value of Money

The value of money is dependent upon the time we need it for. Time of receipt of money, at times, may be more valuable than the amount we receive. This is an important consideration in real estate investing that may at times be hard to liquidate. It is the reason why some people sell their assets below value.

Present Value (PV)

Present Value (PV) shows what future cash flow is worth in terms of present value of dollars. We calculate PV by "discounting" future cash flows by applying "discount rate."

Future Value (FV)

Future Value (FV) – as the name suggests – is the cash flow in the future at a specified time. FV is calculated by applying a given "compound rate" forward in time.

Net Present Value (NPV)

Net Present Value (NPV) tells an investor whether the investment is achieving a target yield based on initial investment: it is the difference between the PV of future cash flows after applying a particular discount rate minus the initial cash invested in purchasing those cash flows.

Net Present Value = Present Value of all Future Cash flows - Initial Cash Investment

NPV Analysis:

- Negative – means the required return on an investment is not met

- Zero – the required return is met as per plan

- Positive – achieved higher than the required return

Internal Rate of Return (IRR)

The internal rate of return (IRR) for an investment property is the percentage rate earned on each dollar invested for each specified period of investment. IRR is also another term people use for interest or yield.

The internal rate of return (IRR) for an investment property is an estimate of the return it generates for each dollar invested during the time frame in which you own it. In simpler terms: IRR is the percentage of interest you earn on each dollar you have invested in a property over the duration of period you hold the property.

For instance, you purchase a retail shop to for a period of 10 years. The compounded interest earned over the 10-year period would represent the IRR.

IRR is a great way to estimate a real estate investment's profitability over a period of time. Unlike Cap Rate, IRR looks beyond the property's net operating income and its purchase price. It gives a clearer picture of expected returns on an investment from start to finish. This is a great tool to analyze profitability of an investment if you are planning to hold it for a long duration.

Formulas for calculating IRR are complex and it is advisable to use an investment calculator or software.

Escrow and Real Estate

Escrow accounts are funds held by a reliable third party to enable the buyer to preform due diligence on a property, assuring the seller they have the capacity to close deal at the end of the stated period. Once the conditions on the sale, such as building inspection or getting satisfactory valuation report are fulfilled, the escrow account holder will release and transfer the payment to the seller. The title of the property is transferred to the buyer.

How to Calculate Rate of Return (ROI) for Real Estate Investments

There are various methods of calculating Return on Investment or ROI of an investment property. In the succeeding paragraphs, we will discuss some of the important ones.

The most common method of calculating Return on investment (ROI) is by using the simple formula:

$$ROI = \frac{Gain\,from\,Investment - Cost\,of\,Investment}{Cost\,of\,Investment}$$

The above equation may look easy to calculate but care needs to be taken to get accurate figures on variables such as repair and maintenance costs, interest on loans, rates, insurances, etc. ROI will be higher if your initial purchase price for the investment is low. Apart from the initial purchase cost, finance cost is another important factor in determining ROI. You must shop for the cheapest loan. Even a small amount of variation in interest rate can have a major implication on ROI.

The Cost Method for Calculating ROI

In the cost method, ROI is calculated by dividing <u>equity in the property</u> by all costs incurred (these include the initial purchase price plus cost of improvements.)

As an example, let us assume that we buy an investment property for $100,000. Let us say that it costs additional $50,000 to carry out repairs and make improvements to the property. On completion of the upgrade, the property valuation comes to $200,000. The investors' <u>equity</u> position in this example will be $50,000. This is arrived at by subtracting the initial purchase cost of $100,000 plus $50,000 repair cost from the revalued price of $200,000.

200,000 - (100,000 + 50,000) = 50,000

ROI from the cost method is arrived at by dividing the equity by all the costs related to the <u>purchase</u>, the upgrade and the repairs in the property.

ROI, in this example, works out to 33% ($50,000 divided by $150,000 multiplied by 100).

The Out of Pocket Method

The Out of Pocket method is very similar to Cost Method but in calculating ROI, only out of pocket cash is taken into account.

Using the same numbers in the example for Cost Method, let us assume that $100,000 purchase was financed taking out a loan in which the <u>down payment</u> was only $20,000. Out of pocket expense in this case will only be $70,000, which includes a down payment of $20,000 plus $50,000 for repairs and upgrade. If the property after rehab is valued at $200,000, the equity will be $130,000.

200,000 - (20,000 + 50,000) = 130,000

The ROI, in this case, will be whopping 185% ($130,000 equity divided by $70,000 out of pocket expenses expressed as a percentage).

The increase in ROI is attributable to leverage applied to the loan by only 20% down payment.

Real estate investors prefer the out-of-pocket method for achieving higher ROI results by applying leverage by putting minimum down payment for the property.

Note of Caution - When calculating ROI, cited in the above examples, care should be taken in adding costs of marketing and brokerage associated with selling. It is also prudent to remember that properties don't always sell at market value. The actual ROI in all probability will be lesser than shown in the example.

ROI will increase if part of the property is tenanted during the rehab process. Rents will add to the cash flow and income.

ROI will also be affected by payment of interest rate during the period of rehab or if the property is refinanced.

The calculations in some cases can become very complex. It is advisable to use investment software /calculators or services of an accountant to arrive at the correct figure.

www.ingramcontent.com/pod-product-compliance
Lightning Source LLC
Chambersburg PA
CBHW020845210326
41598CB00019B/1975